Before You Walk Down the Aisle

A WOMAN'S GUIDE TO SELECTING A LIFELONG PARTNER

What every woman should know before she gets married.

Elizabeth A. Thomas

WESTBOW
PRESS
A DIVISION OF THOMAS NELSON

ISBN: 978-1-4497-2793-2 (sc)
ISBN: 978-1-4497-2794-9 (e)
Library of Congress Control Number: 2011918046

WestBow Press books may be ordered through booksellers or by contacting:

WestBow Press
A Division of Thomas Nelson
1663 Liberty Drive
Bloomington, IN 47403
www.westbowpress.com
1-(866) 928-1240

Because of the dynamic nature of the Internet, any web addresses or links contained in
this book may have changed since publication and may no longer be valid. The views
expressed in this work are solely those of the author and do not necessarily reflect the
views of the publisher, and the publisher hereby disclaims any responsibility for them.

Any people depicted in stock imagery provided by Thinkstock are models,
and such images are being used for illustrative purposes only.
Certain stock imagery © Thinkstock.

Printed in the United States of America
WestBow Press rev. date: 11/09/2011

This book is dedicated to all women: the softer and more emotional of the human species.

A man walking along a California beach was deep in prayer when all of a sudden he said aloud, "Lord grant me one wish." The sky clouded and a booming voice said, "Because you have tried to be faithful I will grant you one wish." The man said, "Build a bridge to Hawaii so I can drive over anytime I want to."

The Lord answered, "Your request is very materialistic. Think of the logistics of that kind of undertaking; the supports required to reach the bottom of the Pacific; the concrete and steel it would take. I can do it, but it is hard for me to justify your desire for worldly things. Take a little more time to think of another wish, a wish you think would honor and glorify me."

The man thought for a long time and finally said, "Lord, I wish that I could understand women. I want to know what they feel inside, what they are thinking when they give me the silent treatment, why they cry, what they mean when they say 'nothing,' and how I can make a woman truly happy." After a long pause God said, "You want two lanes or four on that bridge?"

CONTENTS

AUTHOR'S NOTE

Dear Reader,

The fact that you have chosen to read this book means that you are interested in finding a lifelong partner or you have found that special someone and are considering walking down the aisle. I would like to thank you for taking the time to consider carefully the many issues that relate to the selection of a lifelong partner.

In this guide, I address women in particular, because they are most often the ones who have to respond to the crucial question, "Will you marry me?" As a result, they need to be prepared with the skills to make the right decision. An unhappy marriage is a sure recipe for a miserable life. To ensure that you do not have unhappy reflections about your marriage, you should engage in thoughtful and earnest contemplation now.

As you embark on this experimental journey to find your lover, your best friend, your lifetime partner, your confidant, your baby's daddy, and your forever friend, I pray that you will open your heart and your mind to the Holy Spirit as he leads you into making this important decision.

In this guide you will be required to answer questions. Please answer these questions honestly. This is the only way that you would benefit from the words on these pages. Feel free to read the book as a couple (if you have found that special someone) and discuss the issues that are presented. Have an honest, straightforward talk about your expectations. Write down your thoughts. If you and your partner admit that you have a problem, you may need to seek professional counseling or you may need to reconsider your decision if you are not able to reach a solution.

Sign the promise at the end of some chapters/sections as a reminder of your commitment to each other and to the Lord. If you are reading this book alone, use it to help you to become a desirable lifelong partner. Remember, in marriage, it's not about what you can get, but about what you can give. The spouse that you choose will determine whether you experience a bit of heaven, or a lot of hell, on this Earth.

This is my leap-of-faith project. It was inspired by my passion for a beautiful marriage. When I see a man smile with his entire face as his wife walks into a room, my heart is overjoyed. If I look into his eyes I could almost see his wife's reflection in them. His wife has captured his heart.

The advice and suggestions that will follow are based on my own personal experiences and those of other women that I have conversed with over the years. At the end of the day, you should listen to your own heart and look for someone who matches the ideals that you have set.

May your journey be one that is rewarding and fulfilling. Be Blessed!

After dinner at an American Chinese restaurant some years ago, I was given a fortune cookie that said: "Marriage makes you annoy one person for the rest of your life." The humor of this phrase is lost in the fact that marriage is not forced upon us (well, not upon most of us).

"Will you take this man to be your lawfully wedded husband…till death do you part?"

"I do," replies the excited, blushing bride, for the second time. The first time she said "I do" was in response to "Will you marry me?" It is only fitting that I speak to my female counterparts directly because you are mainly the ones who will be swept off your feet at the altar. Therefore, it's important that you prepare yourself to answer this question correctly—the first time.

According to Jennifer Baker of the Forest Institute of Professional Psychology in Springfield, Missouri, 50 percent of first marriages, 67 percent of second marriages, and 74 percent of third marriages end in divorce. Based on these statistics, your best chance of a successful marriage seems to be best the first time around. For this reason, it is imperative that you make the correct decision.

Marriage was originally designed by God to be a lifetime union between a man and a woman. On the sixth day, God made the animals and man, in the form of Adam. Adam named every species of fish, birds, amphibians, mammals, and insects. The animals were in pairs: male and female. The stallion had its mare, the bull had its cow, the cock had a hen, and the buck had its doe. He observed that there was no animal suitable for him. He was alone.

God may have planned it this way so that Adam would feel a sense of loneliness which could only be filled by a female companion. *"It is* not good that the man should be alone; I will make him an help meet for him" (Genesis 2:18). So God caused a deep sleep to fall upon Adam, and he took a rib from his side and made the helpmeet. When Adam saw what God had made, he described her as "bone of my bone, and flesh of my flesh." He called her "woman, for she was taken out of man" (Genesis 2:23).

The term helpmeet in the authorized King James Version of the Bible (1611) means "a help suitable for him." The Message Bible translates a helpmeet to mean a helper, a companion. I find the new King James Version more appealing—a helpmeet is to be a "helper comparable to him." In other words, God wanted male and female to work together, to support each other, and to complement each other. They were one in God's image. God said "Let us make man in our own image" (Genesis 1:26). They were made in his likeness. The female had one half of God's characteristics, and the male had the other half. When they came together in a sexually intimate way, they became lifelong mates and were whole in God. They became one in marriage.

How do we go about finding this perfect lifelong mate, this perfect helpmeet? God made the choice for Adam, and he can do the same for you. To find that perfect mate, we need to seek counsel from God. We need to receive His approval of our decision.

In the case of Isaac and Rebekah, a praying father and a faithful servant were all it took to accomplish this. Abraham and his servant, Eliezer, trusted God to choose the perfect wife for Isaac. As Eliezer sat at the well of water, near the city of Nahor, he prayed:

> May it be that when I say to a girl, "Please let down your jar that I may drink," and she says, "Drink, and I'll water your camels too"—let her be the one you have chosen for your servant Isaac.(Genesis 24:14)

Before the words were out of his mouth, Rebekah came to the well and the scene played out just as Eliezer had prayed. God is in the business of answering our prayers about our choice of a lifelong partner. He did it for men of old, and he can do it for you too.

The lifelong partner we select can make our marriage difficult and challenging if we choose the wrong person. I am not advocating that a marriage needs to be perfect. Or even that a marriage can be perfect. All marriages require hard work and commitment. In marriage we will experience moments of joy and seasons of heartache. However, if we take the time to get to know each other and to discuss what we expect from a marriage before we get married, we could be spared these seasons of heartache and grief. The important thing is to do everything within our power to make the right choice, and then be willing to work through the difficult times that will definitely arise.

It has been said that the choices we make based on feelings and emotions can lead to greater happiness than choices we make using the cerebral cortex of the brain. This may be true if one is buying a cat or a dog. You may see the cat or the dog and immediately feel a bond. You feel that "this is the one," or you may feel that "this is not the one." Either way, we sometimes permit our hearts to choose for us. We meet someone for the first time and we have a good feeling about him or her. Many women have made friends and enemies using this phenomenon. Unfortunately, if we get to know people long enough we come to realize that our "feelings" were totally erroneous. Sometimes the longer we know someone, the more we admire their ways or the more we dislike their ways. Familiarity breeds admiration or contempt. Don't get me wrong, there is power in women's intuition. However, it becomes futile in our efforts to secure a lifelong partner.

Women were created to love naturally, while men sometimes need to learn to love. This can be understood in the words of Jesus admonishing men to love their wives and women to respect their husbands. As women, we allow our hearts to rule over reason.

How then do we choose the perfect mate? One approach is to learn from the experience of other married couples. What factors were considered before they said "I do"? After being married for a few years, do women generally feel that they have made the right decision? If they were to do it all over again, would they marry the same person?

Answers to these questions can only be obtained when we analyze and scrutinize the experience of married couples. The Japanese have a saying: *hito no furi mite ewaga furi naose*, which means, "learn by yourself, not by what others do." This saying could not be further from the truth in a marriage relationship. We can learn a lot by observing the experiences of others.

The great Roman leader, Julius Caesar, recorded the first known version of the proverb *Experience is the teacher of all things*. Frances M.

Whitcher said, *Experience is the best teacher.* Over the years, many other changes have been made to the proverb. However, the general meaning has remained the same: more people learn by doing something than by reading about it.

My view is very different with respect to experience. My version of this proverb is: **The best teacher is the experience of others.** This gives the proverb a new meaning: more people will learn from the experience of others than by doing it themselves.

We must have within ourselves the qualities that we seek in another. So if you have not yet found that someone special, use this guide as a roadmap to developing the qualities that will make you a suitable lifelong partner. If you have found that special someone, this guide may help you determine if you have made the correct choice. Do not use it as a weapon in your relationship—especially if you have already thought about ending the relationship. I would not have any satisfaction in knowing that I assisted in breaking up a "good thing" or even a "not-so- good thing."

The Woman's Guide to Love and Lasting Relationships:

1. *Find a man who makes you laugh*
2. *Find a man who has a good job and can cook*
3. *Find a man who is honest*
4. *Find a man who will pamper you with gifts*
5. *Find a man who knows what to do in the bedroom*
6. *Most of all, it is very important that these five men never meet!*

Author Unknown

CHAPTER ONE

Why Do Women Get Married?

As I contemplated writing this book, I heard the following dialogue on a local radio program: "I am requesting prayer for my troubled marriage." The caller continued. "My husband loves me very much. He expresses his love in words and actions, but I do not love him. I am having difficulty reciprocating his love," said the caller in a low soft tone. "We have discussed my feelings for him and I have been trying very hard to return his love."

Did I hear the caller correctly? How could you have a husband who loves you and shows you that he loves you, but you do not love him? What happened to this marriage? Why did she marry him in the first place? Did she *ever* love him? These and many more questions plagued my mind as I made a mental note to pray for this couple, especially the wife.

With most real life experiences, if one person feels a particular way, it is very possible that there are many others who feel the same way. Also, if one marriage is dealing with an issue, many others may be experiencing the same problem. So I shared this story with the women in my book club and was very surprised to discover that these older, wiser women had heard similar stories, stories of women who were married and claimed that they were no longer in love with their husbands.

Is it that women get married for the wrong reasons, or do they marry the wrong person? Do women convince themselves that marriage will make them happy? Do they look at this man as their knight in shining armor who would take all their problems away? What if they do choose that perfect person (especially after reading this book)? Is there any guarantee that they will still be in love five...ten...fifteen...thirty... fifty years later?

There is no assurance that a marriage can last "till death do us part." However, with the help of God we can make the first step by choosing someone who is compatible with us. We then need to be determined to work on our marriage. We need to invest time and effort in order to have a successful marriage. So, before you walk down the aisle and say "I do," ask yourself:

Why am I getting married, or Why do I want to get married?"
(write your honest answer here)

_____

_____

_____

_____

_____

_____

_____

_____

Here are six additional reasons that women admit factor into their decision to get married (in no particular order):

1. He is a spiritual person
2. You want to leave your parents' house
3. You are pregnant
4. Your biological clock is ticking
5. He makes you happy
6. It's better to marry than to burn

Promise: I promise to seek God's help in choosing a spouse.

He is a spiritual person

Finding someone who is very spiritual is an excellent reason for getting married. A person who is spiritual will seek the face of God. They will invest time in their relationship with God. Spirituality, however, is not synonymous with religion. It is not measured by church attendance or knowledge of biblical doctrines. Many people attempt to substitute these qualities for a relationship with Christ.

How can you tell if a person is truly spiritual? Only time will tell. The more time we spend together the more capable we become at determining the level of spirituality in other people. I would like to suggest a few elements that we can look for over time:

- Someone who shares what Jesus has provided him; someone who will share thoughts from his devotional time or testimonies of how Jesus has answered his prayers

- Someone who shares the influence scripture has on his life

- Someone who will pray with you and also pray in public; a person whose life is committed to bible study and prayer will have a successful prayer life

- Someone who will engage in praise and worship with you; this may be in private or at a church gathering

- Someone who takes part in a ministry that serves others; this may include volunteering at a homeless shelter, visiting people in hospitals or nursing homes, or volunteering to help young people

We also need to develop ourselves spiritually. What we want to see in others, we must be ourselves. *"Can two walk together, except they be agreed?"* (Amos 3:3). You deserve a man who is a genuine Christian. One who balances his church life, social life, family life, and his work life. When we rush into relationships too quickly, we do not give ourselves time to see the true spiritual side of others.

Promise: I will develop a close relationship with God so that my spiritual life can be one that would please him.

You want to leave your parents' house

Young people leave their parents' house to move forward and become independent adults. However, recent statistics highlight the fact that nowadays in the United States, more young people are returning to live under the roof of their parents after they graduate from college. In other cultures, young people live with their parents until they get married.

You may find yourself wanting to get married to leave home if your relationship with your parents or your siblings is dysfunctional. In the event that this is your predicament, you may need to reconsider your decision to get married. If you cannot get along with the people that you have known for all your life, how do you expect to get along with a husband that you have known for two or three years? It is not going to be very long after you say I do that you will have to deal with some of the same issues that troubled you in your previous home. We take our problems and baggage with us wherever we go. When we get to our destination, we open our bags, unpack, and relive our problems. If you are not happy at home with your parents and you have unresolved issues, please try to resolve them before you say I do. Seek the help of a professional counselor. You may just need to get some things off your chest. You may need to simply say, "I'm sorry" to someone who you have hurt. Or maybe you just need to hear them say, "I'm sorry" to you.

Whatever you do, don't bury your baggage; don't bury your past. It will not decay. At some point in time it will be disturbed and resurface.

Promise: I promise to leave my father and mother and to cleave to my spouse only if I have a good relationship with them.

You are pregnant

Children are an inheritance from the Lord. Children are a blessing to any family. Psalm 127: 3 says:

> *Lo, children are an heritage of the LORD: and the fruit of the womb is his reward.*

In the event that you get pregnant before you walk down the aisle, please do not marry before the baby comes to save face. Getting married will not make the sin of sex before marriage right. Your pregnancy will not be considered more acceptable if you get married.

During the 2008 presidential elections in the United States, the unmarried daughter of a vice-presidential candidate admitted to being pregnant. The couple were both still in high school. The young man said that he was willing to drop out of school and find a job to support his family. Fortunately for them, they decided to call off the wedding, stating that marriage was not the best option at the time. Hats off to them! They probably (no, definitely) spared themselves many years of unnecessary stress, strain, and conflict.

An unplanned pregnancy can sometimes put a strain on a successful marriage; just imagine what it will do to a struggling marriage or to a marriage that was rushed into. Getting married when you are not prepared emotionally or financially is not conducive to a long-lasting relationship, and usually, this is the case when you get married because of a baby. Do yourself and your child's father a favor—save the wedding, should you decide that's the best thing for all of you, for the day your child can be your ring bearer or flower girl. It will be worth it.

Sharing a child is not reason enough to walk down the aisle. If you don't believe me, ask yourself, "What do I have to lose by waiting?" Nothing! Then wait.

Promise: I promise that I will not use pregnancy as a reason to get married.

_____

Your biological clock is ticking

Research shows that the average woman's ability to get pregnant begins to slow down as early as age thirty. As a woman gets older, she releases fewer eggs, and those eggs are less easily fertilized. However, in a society where medical technology is so advanced, a woman need not be very concerned about her biological clock. There are options for older women who want to become mothers.

A woman can have her eggs harvested and preserved for later use. When she is ready, the egg can be fertilized and implanted in her uterus or the uterus of another woman, called a surrogate mother, by a process known as in vitro fertilization.

There is also the option of adoption. The United States Department of Health and Human Services report of 2010, notes that there are over 100,000 in the public foster care waiting to be adopted. There are also countless others that can be adopted "legally" from outside of the United States. Adopted children have brought much happiness and joy to many couples, and similarly, many couples have brought joy and happiness to adopted children. When a child is adopted, a new birth certificate is made and the names of the adopted parents are included in the birth paper.

He makes you happy

> *"My wife and I were happy for 20 years, then we met!"*
> *-Rodney Dangerfield*

Happiness is defined as the quality or state of being delighted or pleased with something or someone. It is not synonymous with a life devoid of problems, but is reflective of a life that values overcoming problems. There are occasions when we allow ourselves to live under circumstances that are unpleasant, so that we remain unhappy. The following story illustrates this.

One beautiful summer day I decided to go for a walk. Since I was home alone, I had to take my house keys with me. My exercise clothes did not have any pockets, so I decided to put the keys in my socks. As I began my five-mile walk, I felt the keys rubbing annoyingly against my ankle. At first, I was able to bear the discomfort, but after a few minutes it became unbearable.

It finally dawned on me that maybe I could try to adjust the keys. So I stopped, bent over, and shifted the keys in my socks. I stood up and began to walk again. The keys still felt annoying and uncomfortable. I stopped again, and shifted the keys once more. I began walking again. This time the discomfort was gone. I had shifted the keys correctly.

We all have "keys" that make us uncomfortable. Sometimes we can live with the discomfort and other times we cannot. It may take us a while to figure out that all we need to do is to stop, rethink the situation, and adjust to relieve our pain and enjoy the happiness that life has to offer.

Unfortunately, some of us never find this happiness. One of my friends was asked by her therapist to share a time in her life when she was happy. Before she could answer, she had to ask the therapist what happiness felt like. She had been unhappy for such a long time that she could not recall feelings of happiness.

Someone who creates an environment that breeds happiness is truly a blessing to be around. Someone who is able to bring a smile to your face is a beautiful thing. However, we must always have our smile with us. Our happiness need not be centered on one person or thing. The church is a place where we go to worship Jesus, but we do not meet Jesus at church, we take him to church with us. It is the same with happiness. We need to be happy and take our happiness with us so that we will be a blessing to others. As it was once said, "Happiness held is the seed; happiness shared is the flower" (source unknown).

Recently, I was privileged to see first-hand the Summer Palace, where the Emperor, Empress, and his many concubines lived. In the palace of the emperor was a Chinese symbol of marriage that represents double happiness. One part represents the happiness that the male brings to the relationship, and the other represents the happiness that the female brings. When they come together, they symbolize 'double happiness'. In ancient China and even today, the phoenix is used as the symbol of happiness for the female, and the dragon for the male. These two symbols are used to represent the happiness that each person brings to a marriage.

God wants us to find joy in our marital relationship with one another. The more permanent side of happiness is joy. Happiness is based on what's happening around us, but joy is rooted in knowing the Lord and having a relationship with him.

Promise: I promise to be happy and filled with joy despite what comes my way.

It's better to marry than to burn

In 1 Corinthians 7:9, the Bible says:

> *"However, if you cannot control your desires, you should get married. It is better for you to marry than to burn [with sexual desire]." God's Word Translation (1995)*

This admonition though, must be taken within the context of finding a suitable lifelong partner. I believe the Apostle Paul did not mean for us to marry the first man that we meet if we are 'burning' with passion. Notice that the first part of the text said that 'if you cannot contain your desires'. Paul was a proponent of abstinence. Many people believe that it is best to practice abstinence before marriage."

While I was writing this section, Rebecca St. James, Grammy Award–winning Christian singer, married Jacob Fink, the man of her dreams. The couple exchanged their purity rings and washed each other's feet. The washing of the feet symbolized their commitment to serve each other. Rebecca has been an advocate of purity for many years and has encouraged many young women to remain pure and virtuous until marriage.

Remaining pure in a premarital relationship is crucial to the success of a marriage. Sexual intercourse has its place only in marriage. The first couple, Adam and Eve, was married, and we have reason to believe that sex was an integral part of their relationship. This probably opened up a new dimension of pleasure for them both that they never would have experienced had they remained single.

Couples may feel that they need to have sex before they are married to determine if they are sexually compatible. But the truest test of compatibility might be sharing a checkbook!

Sex is not the same as buying a car—we don't have to test drive it to know if it's working well. Sexual compatibility is determined by the level of spirituality of the couple, the couples' awareness of the purpose of sex, and their expectations regarding sex in marriage.

If a couple does engage in sex before marriage and decide to get married, they need to make a concerted effort to remain pure until the wedding.

> *Do you not know that your body is the temple of the Holy*
> *Spirit, who is in you, whom you have received from God? You*
> *are not your own; you were bought at a price.*
> *Therefore honor God with your body.*
> (1 Cor. 6:19-20) NIV

CHAPTER TWO

The Number One Reason for Getting Married

Do what makes you happy, Be with who makes you smile,
Laugh as much as you breathe, Love as long as you live.
—Unknown

I love cheesecake, I love chocolate cake, I love burrito bowls, I love tofu hot-dogs, and I love my husband. Hmm… Something doesn't belong. Which one is different—do you know? Can you guess which of these things is not like the other? If you guessed "my husband," you are correct. Can I, should I, talk about my loving husband in the same breath as cheesecake, chocolate cake, and a burrito bowl? What is love?

Webster's Dictionary describes love as a "profoundly tender, passionate affection for another person." This affection grows as it is fostered and nourished. There are three types of love: eros, philos, and agape. Eros love is the love we have for someone when we first meet them. We see them and we approve of what we see. Philos love is love that is built on eros love. At this level, our relationship is able to withstand the strains and stresses of life. Agape love is unconditional love; it is love despite what the other person does. This is the kind of love that Jesus has for us. Love beyond all human reason.

The number one reason for getting married is **love**. Love is the foundation of a marriage. A psychologist recently shared his view on marriages that have been affected and infected with infidelity. He theorized that these marriages could be viable if the couple stayed focused on the fact that they loved each other. As the popular 80's song by Captain and Tenille said, "Love will keep us together." This might be true if both parties share these similar loving feelings. The challenge arises when one or both parties are no longer in love with each other or have hurt each other to the extent that love "cannot cover a multitude of sins."

King Solomon's description of love is epitomized in the following Bible passage from **Proverbs 30:18-19**:

> *There are three things that amaze me—*
> *no, four things that I don't understand:*
> *how an eagle glides through the sky,*
> *how a snake slithers on a rock,*
> *how a ship navigates the ocean,*
> *how a woman loves a man.* *(NLT)*

> *The story is told of a blind girl who hated herself just because she was blind. She hated everyone, except her loving boyfriend. He was always there for her. She said that if she could only see the world, she would marry her boyfriend. One day, someone donated a pair of eyes to her and then she could see everything, including her boyfriend. Her boyfriend asked her, "now that you can see the world, will you marry me?" The girl was shocked when she saw that her boyfriend was blind too, and refused to marry him. Her boyfriend walked away in tears, and later wrote a letter to her saying..... "Just take care of my eyes dear." I'll always love you forever.*

How do we know when we are in love? Actors have made a fortune over the years trying to demonstrate this thing called love. Hollywood stories are incomplete without a heart-warming romance—even G-rated movies depict romance among species in the animal kingdom.

To love someone is a decision that we make. We have to willingly open our hearts to the person. Sometimes our heart opens for us, due to the fact that it has a mind of its own. You meet someone for the first time and there's an instant connection that you can only explain to someone who has also experienced it. The irrepressible butterflies that we feel in our stomachs sometimes suggest the beginnings of love.

When you are in love, you can tell when the other person is happy or sad. You hear happiness or sadness in their voice, without even seeing their face. You speak to each other with the eyes. (If you find yourself smiling as you read this, you might very well be remembering your own experiences; if you are not smiling, don't worry—one day you will.) You feel you have become a better person because they are in your life. Seeing them makes you forget all the bad things that may have happened to you during the course of a day. When this is your experience, your love has reached the philos stage.

Another sign of love is being aware of someone's bad habits and still being able to smile, knowing that you can live with them. Our mothers may get on our last nerve with their traditional ways, but they are still our mothers, and we love them unconditionally. Our sisters will wear our favorite blouse and don't get it cleaned in time for us to wear it. We may get upset, but we don't leave her; we deal with it and move on. She apologizes, promises never to do it again and breaks her promise. But it's all good; it is something that you can live with. You love her. You now love at the agape level of the love triangle.

Adam and Eve experienced this kind of agape love. It is what I believe contributed to the entrance of sin to our world. Adam made a conscious decision to eat the fruit from the Tree of Knowledge, of Good and Evil knowing that he would die. After all, God had said, *"In the day that you eat of the tree you will surely die."* But Adam loved Eve so much that he chose to die with her rather than to live without her. What Adam did not realize was that God loved him more and would have provided a way out. He may have replaced Eve with someone far more beautiful and lovable than Eve.

Isn't it ironic: love bred hate, murder, and all other sins. Is it any wonder that a marriage that starts out with love sometimes boils down to hate when two people remove themselves from the source of love? When two people no longer place God as the center of their relationship, sin steps in as it did in the Garden of Eden. Eve chose to place the Tree of Knowledge at the center of her life. Sin stepped in when Adam placed Eve at the center of his life.

The openness that I hope you and your future spouse develop as a result of reading this book is vital to the development and maintenance of a successful marriage. I know that men shy away from discussions of this nature, but we can encourage them to share their feelings if we choose the right time and place to do so. Sharing feelings may also be a cultural thing. In some cultures, men don't talk about their feelings; they learn to keep them inside. We have to teach men how important it is for them to share their feelings.

Love can be expressed in words and actions. God loved us even more, and showed his love by sending his son, Jesus, to die for our sins so that we could go to heaven, rather than to live without us.

In Gary Chapman's book The *Five Love Languages*, he notes that, "There are five ways that humans express love; but for each of us, while all five ways might be appealing to us, only two or three actually make us FEEL loved. We need to be loved; but more specifically, each of us needs to be loved in one or two of these particular love languages.

The five languages are:

1. Words of affirmation - hearing encouragement, promises of loyalty and love
2. Quality time – spending time with loved ones
3. Receiving Gifts – giving a gift as a sign of love
4. Acts of service – serving others
5. Physical touch - cuddles and hugs

I close this chapter with the words of the Apostle Paul found in 1 Corinthians 13:1–13:

> *If I speak in the tongues of men or of angels, but do not have love, I am only a resounding gong or a clanging cymbal. If I have the gift of prophecy and can fathom all mysteries and all knowledge, and if I have a faith that can move mountains, but do not have love, I am nothing. If I give all I possess to the poor and give over my body to hardship that I may boast¹ but do not have love, I gain nothing.*

> *Love is patient, love is kind. It does not envy, it does not boast, it is not proud. It does not dishonor others, it is not self-seeking, it is not easily angered, it keeps no record of wrongs. Love does not delight in evil but rejoices with the truth. It always protects, always trusts, always hopes, always perseveres.*

Love never fails. But where there are prophecies, they will cease; where there are tongues, they will be stilled; where there is knowledge, it will pass away. For we know in part and we prophesy in part, but when completeness comes, what is in part disappears. When I was a child, I talked like a child, I thought like a child, I reasoned like a child. When I became a man, I put the ways of childhood behind me. For now we see only a reflection as in a mirror; then we shall see face to face. Now I know in part; then I shall know fully, even as I am fully known.

And now these three remain: faith, hope and love. But the greatest of these is love.

Promise: I will get married to someone whom I **love**.

_____

CHAPTER THREE

Whom Should You Marry?

Over the years I've people-watched and have made certain assumptions about the relationships of couples I've observed. In this chapter, I share some these assumptions. Remember, the key is to learn from the mistakes and successes of others. You should marry...

Someone who shares your love for the Lord

Marsha and Bob had had a major argument earlier in the day. They are now seated at the dinner table, in silence. Thinking about how much he loves his wife, Bob reached over and laid a hand on Marsha's shoulder. He felt a deep sense of love and togetherness. Marsha, sensed his feelings and drew closer to him. He held her closer and prayed, "Dear Father, I want to thank you for bringing Marsha into my life. She is the joy of my life. Thank you for the blessings you have given us a couple. Forgive me for hurting Marsha. Teach us to love each other as you have loved us. Help me to love, honor, and respect Marsha." Marsha whispered, "Dear Father, I thank you for Bob. I thank you that he provides for our family. Help me to respect and love him. Forgive me for hurting Bob. Bind us together with cords of love that can never be broken." Bob reached over, held his wife's face and said, "I love you, my sweet beauty, please forgive me." Marsha replied, "You forgive me. I adore you, my prince." They kissed in a way that only the presence of the Holy Spirit could have inspired.

Spiritual compatibility is an important aspect of a successful marriage. Being able to share moments of deep connection with God forms a bond between husband and wife that aids in binding their hearts together. These deep connections come from spending time together engaged in the work of the Lord or serving others. This bond becomes a powerful tool for sharing the gospel and inspiring other couples.

Tom and Mary both serve as leaders of the children's group at their local church. They sponsor outings and supervise the children as they engage in community service activities. They also teach the children Bible lessons every week at the church. They have said that they have grown to love the kids with whom they work, and they also fell more deeply in love with each other as they work together.

Someone who is faithful to you

Current statistics reveal that 30 to 60 percent of all married persons in the United States will engage in an extramarital affair at some point during their marriage. Infidelity in any form or fashion has a devastating effect on the success of a marriage. Henry and Michelle's marriage experienced, and fortunately, survived infidelity.

They had dated for one year before Henry confessed that he had been involved in a sexual affair with a young lady on his job six months after his relationship with Michelle had started. Michelle was devastated. She considered ending the relationship, but loved Henry very much. She decided to forgive Henry. They never discussed the matter again. They were married two years later.

It would be ideal if their story had a happy ending, but after ten years of marriage and one child, Henry was unfaithful again. This time he engaged in an emotional affair. Henry shared his story with Michelle a year after he discontinued the relationship. He told her that he did not engage in sexual intercourse with the other woman, but had had a romantic, emotional relationship with her nonetheless. Michelle felt hurt and betrayed. She knew that she had to make a choice. Michelle contemplated divorcing Henry, but loved him too much to do so. With the help of God, Michelle decided that she would stay with Henry on the condition that they seek counseling. Henry agreed. They spent the next two years undergoing marriage counseling. Henry sought help from a sex therapist because he had unresolved issues from his childhood that he discovered were at the root of his problem. They spent two years in therapy and were able to reconcile and save their marriage.

As Michelle reflected on her marriage, she came to realize that they should have sought counseling before marriage. These sessions would have given them the opportunity to share their expectations of marriage, including sexual expectations. They would have discussed Henry's premarital transgression, and perhaps they could have been spared the heartache they had experienced for more than ten years.

Michelle and Henry's story is not unique. Many marriages are affected by infidelity in one form or another. The early signs of infidelity can be seen in the following scenario I witnessed at a church picnic a few years ago. A young lady dressed in a pair of jeans walked across the grass. Like a porsche, she had all the curves in right places. The eyes of a married brother followed her across the lawn until she sat down. His wife's eyes followed her husband's as he followed the young lady's voluptuous hips. The wife stared blankly at her husband, with a look on her face that spoke volumes to the fact that this was not her husband's first "staring" episode. In the five seconds it took for this situation to unfold, I saw a woman broken by the infidelity of her husband. Broken by the trust that was severed by his adulterous behavior.

The infidelity in this case took place in the mind of the man. We can blame the young lady for wearing a pair of jeans that showed her curves, or we could remind the man that "birds will always fly over his head, but he can prevent them from making a nest in his hair." As simple and commonplace as this incident may seem, it is a very debilitating force in a marriage. I'm not referring here to a man who looks at a beautiful, attractive woman—even women admire other beautiful, well-dressed women. This is about the man who frequently stares at women. It shows that he has wandering, lustful eyes and maybe engaging in emotional (or physical) affairs.

In Matthew 5:28, the Bible says, *"I tell you that anyone who looks at a woman lustfully has already committed adultery with her in his heart."* Wandering eyes say a lot about a person's earlier experiences and habits they may have formed over the years. I remember dialoguing with an eighteen-year-old young man once and condoning the fact that men had a natural inclination to stare at women. His response baffled me. He suggested that men trained themselves to be this way. It wasn't until years later that I realized he was correct.

It seems that some men engage in this activity regularly until it becomes a habit. A friend of mine shared with me that her husband had developed this propensity by looking at ladies through a tinted glass window with his friends after work. They would scrutinize the ladies as they strolled passed the glass window. Now, years later, he is struggling to get over this habit.

I think it is insulting to a woman if the man she is with stares at another woman in her presence. If this is a concern with your potential lifelong partner, bring it to his attention. If you are embarrassed to do so, use this section of the book as a springboard for your discussion. Be open and honest about how it makes you feel. If he really loves you he will attempt to modify his behavior. Men can change if they want to, especially after they recognize the full impact of their actions.

We often become sad when we hurt someone, but we become heartbroken and distraught when we come to terms with the true cost and consequences of what we have done. Just imagine for a minute that you are invited to your friend's house and you see a very nice vase. You pick it up to admire it and somehow it slips from your grasp. As it falls, your friend's face goes deathly pale. You apologize profusely and promise to buy a replacement at the local store. Your friend, however, appears inconsolable. When she finally speaks, she tells you that the vase had originally belonged to her great-great grandmother and had been passed down to her. It was worth $50,000. Your apologies become moans and groans as you now realize the full cost of what you have done.

Paul in 2 Corinthians 5:17 says, *"Therefore, if anyone is in Christ, he is a new creation; the old has gone, the new has come!"*

Someone who values you as a person

> *"You're beautiful, you are made for so much more than this… you're beautiful, you are treasured, you are sacred, you are his…"*

These are the lyrics to the song 'Beautiful' by the Christian vocal group "Mercy Me." We all need to be told that we are beautiful, treasured, loved, and special. Bruno Mars also echoes the same sentiments in his song "Just the Way You Are":

> *"When I see your face there's not a thing I would change, cause you're amazing, just the way you are. And when you smile, the*

whole world stops and stares for a while, cause you're amazing,
just the way you are."

Anyone who wants to share space in your life must see you as a beautiful person; beautiful enough to value your physical, mental, emotional, and psychological states. You should never feel that you deserve to be spoken to, touched, or treated in a hostile or abusive way. There is **never a reason** for you to be physically abused.

In many relationships there may not be any physical abuse, but there might be emotional abuse. Emotional abuse is a form of abuse characterized by a person subjecting or exposing another to behavior that is psychologically harmful.

A young lady began to lose interest in activities she used to enjoy. She felt guilty, hopeless, and worthless. She ate more and slept little. Her doctor told her that she was showing signs of depression. He inquired as to whether she was under any stress at work. He had ruled out biological causes of stress because she was not experiencing premenstrual problems, pregnancy, infertility issues, or post-partum depression. He then asked about her love life. Was she dissatisfied with her relationship? Based on her responses, the doctor surmised that she was experiencing persistent, psychosocial stressors. These stressors were directly linked to her boyfriend's constant barrage of demeaning and cruel words. Her body was being stressed because it could not respond appropriately to the verbal threats. The doctor advised her to end the relationship and move on with her life. She did. She was eventually healed from her depressive state.

Someone who values you as a person will speak highly of you and bring positivity into your life. Someone who values you as a person will shower you with compliments and words of affirmation. Someone who values you as a person will inspire you to fulfill your greatest potential. This reminds me of the "The Eagle Story" in *Faith in the Night Seasons* by Nancy Missler.

> *The story begins with a wounded eaglet who was rescued by a kind farmer. He found the bird in one of his fields, and so took him home, tended to his wounds, and then placed him outside in the barnyard to recover.*
>
> *Strangely enough, the young eaglet soon adapted to the habits*

of all the barnyard chickens. He learned to walk and cluck like them. He learned to drink from a trough and peck the dirt for food, and for many years he peacefully resigned himself to this new life on the ground.

But then one day, one of the farmer's friends spotted the eagle and asked, "Why in the world is that bird acting like a chicken?" The farmer told him what had happened; yet the man could hardly accept the situation.

"It's just not right," said the friend. "The Creator made that bird to soar in the heavens, not scavenge in the barnyard!" So he picked up the unsuspecting eagle, climbed onto a nearby fence post, and tossed him into the air. But the confused bird just fell back to earth and scurried off in search of his feathered friends.

Undaunted, the man then grabbed the eagle and climbed to the top of the barn. As he heaved him off the roof, the bird made a few halfhearted squawks and flaps before falling into a bale of hay. After shaking his head a few times, the eagle then made himself comfortable and began mindlessly pecking at pieces of straw.

The friend went home that night dejected, and could barely sleep as he remembered the sight of those powerful talons caked with barnyard mud. He couldn't bear the thought, so the very next day, he headed back to the farm for another try. This time he carried the eagle to the top of a nearby mountain where the sky unfolded in a limitless horizon.

He looked into the eagle's eyes and cried out, "Don't you understand? You weren't made to live like a chicken! Why would you want to stay down here when you were born for the sky?" As the man held the confused bird aloft, he made sure the eagle was facing into the brilliant light of the setting sun. Then he powerfully heaved the bird into the sky, and this time the eagle opened his wings, looked at the sun, caught the updraft rising from the valley, and disappeared into the clouds of heaven.

Are you an eagle living like a chicken? Is there a special someone in your life who is willing to pick you up and help you to fly? The people you hold close should do as that farmer's friend, and never give up on you. They should believe in your potential, seek your best interests, and inspire you to do great things.

Someone who values you as a person will love you just the way you are!

A beautiful true love story is told of John Blanchard, a soldier who found a book at a local library that had notes penciled in the margin. The soft handwriting reflected a thoughtful soul and insightful mind. In front of the book, he discovered the previous owner's name, Miss Hollis Maynell. He located her address. She lived in New York City. He wrote her a letter introducing himself and inviting her to correspond. The next day he was shipped overseas for service in World War II. During the next year and one-month the two grew to know each other through the mail. Each letter was a seed falling on a fertile heart. A romance was budding. Blanchard requested a photograph, but she refused. She felt that if he really cared, it wouldn't matter what she looked like.

When the day finally came for him to return from Europe, they scheduled their first meeting—7:00 pm at Grand Central Station in New York.

"You'll recognize me," she wrote, "by the red rose I'll be wearing on my lapel." So at 7:00 he was in the station looking for a girl whose heart he loved, but whose face he'd never seen.

A young woman came toward him, her figure long and slim. Her blond hair lay back in curls from her delicate ears; her eyes were blue as flowers. Her lips and chin had a gentle firmness, and in her pale green suit she was like springtime come alive. He started toward her, entirely forgetting to notice that she was not wearing a rose. As he moved, a small, provocative smile curved her lips. "Going my way, sailor?" she murmured.

Almost uncontrollably he made one step closer to her, and then he saw Hollis Maynell. She was standing almost directly behind the girl. A woman well past 40, she had graying hair tucked under a worn hat. She was more than plump, her thick-ankled feet thrust into low-heeled shoes. The girl in the green suit was walking quickly away. He felt as though he was split in two, so keen was his desire to follow her, and yet so deep was his longing for the woman whose spirit had truly companioned him and upheld his own.

And there she stood. Her pale, plump face was gentle and sensible; her gray eyes had a warm and kindly twinkle. He did not hesitate. His fingers gripped the small worn blue leather copy of the book that was something precious, something perhaps even better than love, a friendship for which he had been and must ever be grateful.

He squared his shoulders and saluted and held out the book to the woman, even though while he spoke he felt choked by the bitterness of his disappointment. "I'm Lieutenant John Blanchard, and you must be Miss Maynell. I am so glad you could meet me; may I take you to dinner?" The woman's face broadened into a tolerant smile. "I don't know what this is about, son," she answered, "but the young lady in the green suit who just went by, she begged me to wear this rose on my coat. And she said if you were to ask me out to dinner, I should go and tell you that she is waiting for you in the big restaurant across the street. She said it was some kind of test!"

The young soldier had passed the test. He showed that he loved Miss Maynell just the way she was.

Someone who is gentle

The old Aesop fable of The North Wind and the Sun demonstrates the quality of gentleness in a special way.

> *The North Wind boasted of great strength. The Sun argued that there was great power in gentleness. "We shall have a contest," said the Sun. Far below, a man traveled a winding road. He was wearing a warm winter coat. "As a test of strength," said the Sun, "Let us see which of us can take the coat off of that man." "It will be quite simple for me to force him to remove his coat," bragged the Wind. The Wind blew so hard, the birds clung to the trees. The world was filled with dust and leaves. But the harder the wind blew down the road, the tighter the shivering man clung to his coat. Then, the Sun came out from behind a cloud. Sun warmed the air and the frosty ground. The man on the road unbuttoned his coat. The sun grew slowly brighter and brighter. Soon the man felt so hot, he took off his coat and sat down in a shady spot. "How did you do that?" said the Wind. "It was easy," said the Sun, "I lit the day. Through gentleness I got my way."*

A man's upbringing may have a significant effect on his ability to display gentleness. In their book *The Love Dare*, Stephen and Alex Kendrick describe being gentle as "being careful about how you treat your spouse, being tender, sensitive and speaking the truth in love."Gentleness means recognizing that people are fragile and we should try not to harm others but choose instead to be tender, soft-spoken, kindhearted, and careful.

When we are gentle we touch the world in ways that protect and preserve it. A man who was taught this quality by his father, mother, or siblings is a rare treasure. As you engage in the getting-to-know-you process, be sure to look for the signs of gentleness in his body language. These include: speech that is soft, kind, and under control, and eyes that are soft, tender, attentive, and concerned. The head is titled forward in your direction to show that he's interested in you. He sits forward leaning his upper body toward you to show that he wants to be close to you.

Someone who has a different personality than yours

The old proverb "opposites attract" has been the basis for the formation of marital relationships. However, as the years progress, these opposite features can become annoying. The spouse who was once spontaneous and adventurous is now seen as irresponsible and childish. The spouse who allowed you to make decisions for him is now viewed as indecisive and weak.

Regardless, there is some truth to opposites attracting. Just imagine how boring life would be if we were all the same. The key to dealing with the effects of the "opposites" is to understand each other. Requiring change in a person's personality or temperament is not the best way to make a relationship work, as a person may change only temporarily to please you. The key to a successful marriage of opposites attracting is for couples to understand one another and use this knowledge to deal with the personality and behavioral differences that may arise.

Marita Littauer, in her book, *Wired that Way*, provides information on the four temperaments: Sanguine, Choleric, Melancholy, and Phelgmatic. These temperaments define how we react to situations. Many experts in the field of personality types are of the view that there is no one perfect temperament. Sanguine people are *expressive*, outgoing, cheerful, and optimistic. Their personality will conflict with that of the Choleric because they are very laidback and wait for things to happen. Cholerics are *dominant*. They do not waste time on activities that they consider to be unimportant. In contrast the Sanguine person can converse with everyone and enjoy the conversation. Melancholy people are *analytical*. They think before they speak and act. They are perfectionists. They have been known to have a very poor self-image. Phelgmatics are strong and *solid*. They are often content to spend time by themselves. They are enthusiastic about life.

Each individual has both a strong and a weak personality, and we all have some characteristics in common. As Tim LaHaye said in his book, *Spirit-Controlled Temperament*, "No one temperament can be said to be better than another. Each one contains strengths and richness, yet each one is fraught with its own weaknesses and dangers." Similarly, Littauer recommends that we marry someone who has at least "one square" in common with us.

God could have made us all Expressives.
We could have lots of fun but accomplish little.
He could have made us all Analyticals.
We would have been organized and charted
but not very cheerful.
He could have made us all Dominants.
We would have been set to lead,
but impatient that no one would follow!
He could have made us all Solids.
We would have had a peaceful world
but not much enthusiasm for life.
We need each temperament for the total function of the body.
Each part should do its work to unify the action
and produce harmonious results.

–Florence Littauer in *The Gift of Encouraging Words*

Myers & Briggs have also provided us with information on the personality types of people by using a more elaborate perspective. They define personality as four basic dichotomies: extrovert versus introvert; sensors versus intuitive; thinkers versus feelers; judgers versus perceivers. These dichotomies are then grouped into sixteen distinctive blends.

In a marriage, we need the person who is an extrovert to support the person who is an introvert. Sensors' practical way of looking at things is ideally suited with that of the intuitive person, often known as the dreamer. A person who is a thinker uses logic to deal with situations, while feelers are very emotional and are always concerned with the feelings of others. Judgers are perfectionists. They are the workaholics. The flip side of this is perceivers. They are very flexible and not as concerned about completing projects.

Whether you decide to use the personality types that Littauer embraces or the Myers-Briggs Personality Types, you should consider using this information to understand your potential partner and then work toward accepting the person for who they are.

Someone who is unselfish

Romans 12:10 says,

> *"Be devoted to one another in brotherly love; give*
> *preference to one another in honor."*

A baby cries if it is wet, hungry, sleepy, or lonely; you name it, and a baby cries for it. A baby is consumed with itself. It is not concerned about the fact that the mother is tired, hungry, or sleepy. Babies are, by nature, helpless creatures. This is their defense mechanism. This is the way they get our attention so that we can take care of them. They put their interests, desires, and priorities above that of everyone else.

This is natural, expected, and okay for a baby, but when an adult displays these qualities it is construed as selfishness. Selfish love thinks only of itself. It covets what others have. Selfishness could lead to adultery and fornication. A truly unselfish person will take care of the needs of others, especially the needs of those they claim to love. He or she will want the best for their partner; he or she will want them to feel loved and will have their best interest at heart. Unselfishness in a relationship is portrayed when two people try to out-give each other.

CHAPTER FOUR

Before You Say "I Do"

Before you say "I do," ask yourself the following questions:

1. **Do I really know the person that I am marrying? Write ten things you know about the person.**

_____

_____

_____

_____

_____

_____

_____

_____

_____

_____

_____

_____

_____

If you had difficulty coming up with ten very positive and significant things you may want to consider waiting before you say I do. How long should you wait? Long enough to get to know the person in various situations. Long enough to get to know those who knew him before you did. Long enough for these people to share intimate details about the person with you. These details could possibly expose habits that you may not be able to live with or habits that you may want to discuss with your partner before you walk down the aisle. Remember, we grew up with our siblings and parents, and they still do things that annoy us. Give your relationship time for your partner to get on your nerves and pay attention to how you deal with it. Give yourself time, time, and more time.

You may ask the question, "Why wait when you are sure that it was a match made in heaven?" If it is truly a match made in heaven, remember that heaven keeps no record of time. The Bible tells us in 2 Peter 3: 8, *"a day is like a year for our Lord."* So, wait.

You may know of people that courted for a short period before they got married and their marriage was successful. You may also hear of courtships that were more than two years long and the ensuing marriages failed. Ted Huston, Ph.D., a professor of psychology and human ecology at the University of Texas at Austin, has collected data on 168 couples since 1979. In his study, he has found that couples that dated for more than a year were more happily married. Hudson's study found that couples who did not date exclusively before marriage divorced after two to seven years of marriage. So learn from the experiences of others and give your relationship time. The experiences of others should be used as a window into the future. All you will lose by waiting is time. So wait!

2. **What are my views on sharing work in a marriage? Is it a woman's job to cook, clean, do laundry, and take care of the kids, or should household chores be shared?**

_____

_____

_____

_____

_____

_____

_____

_____

Household chores may prove to be a conflicting subject. The chores must be done, therefore, it would be useful to have this discussion and decide who does what: the wife, the husband, or the maid.

3. Is there anything that I don't like about my potential partner and may not want/be able to to deal with?

_____

_____

_____

_____

_____

_____

_____

The following is a list of common concerns or conflicts that occur in marriage:

- Workaholic– Someone who works all the time, is always in school, or is always engaged in activities that consume his time. Couples must spend time together so that their relationship can grow and strengthen. If your potential partner is busy most of the time, this may continue after you are married, and the marriage may be strained because the only time that you will see each other is when you are tired.

- Debt - He may not readily share this information with you; you may have to ask to see credit reports. Remember, the credit ratings of husbands and wives can affect each other.

- Money Management – You may be one to save your money and buy cash whereas your partner may want to buy everything on credit. Conflict over money is one of the top five reasons for divorce.

- In-laws – If your relationship with your in-laws is not close, you may have to decide if you can live with that. It would mean that your children would not know the pleasure of doting grandparents and the joy of playing with cousins. If your in-laws are overly protective of your partner and have an input into matters that do not concern them, you may need to decide if you can live with that as well.

- Jealousy– If your partner does not give you room to breathe, this may be unhealthy. You ought to engage in some activities without him. Love can cause one to become extremely protective, but when that love becomes suffocating it is a cause for concern.

- Alcohol and substance abuse – These not only kill a marriage but can also take lives. If you feel that you can help a person through the rehabilitation process, make sure there are visible signs of change as these habits may worsen over time. Make certain you are willing to live with the consequences if the intervention does not work.

- Pornography – If your potential partner is involved in pornography, please encourage him to get help. Pornography can destroy the relationship between a husband and a wife. It is a disastrous form of adultery. The wife is left to feel rejected, inadequate, ugly, and undesirable. Talk to your partner and encourage him to seek counseling.

- Infidelity – Every day the media is filled with stories of husbands who have been unfaithful to their wives. Studies conducted reveal that 23 to 68 percent of men and 15 to 66 percent of women have engaged in infidelity or adultery. In many of these cases, the infidelity began before marriage.

4. Do we communicate positively with each other?

Merriam-Webster's online dictionary defines communication as a process by which information is exchanged between individuals through a common system of symbols or signs or behavior. Communication therefore is both receptive and expressive. It is how we listen and what we say in words, actions and body language. Communication can be both negative and positive. Negative communication destroys whereas positive communication builds up.

1. Are you and your partner able to discuss problems without hurting each other's feelings? Do you allow problems to escalate or are you or your partner able to 'defuse' contentious issues? Do you feel hurt and wounded after you have communicated with or partner? Do you hurt or wound your partner? We should never allow our communication to be so negative that when we do speak lovingly to our partner, they are unable to feel or accept our love.

2. Does your partner listen to you with sincerity and speak to you with respect? This does not mean that everything we say will be understood the way it was meant to be, there may be times when our words and actions may be misunderstood. However, these occasions should be few and if we have been in the habit of communicating positively, our partner will ask for clarification on what we have shared.

3. Do you or your partner avoid discussing issues that you perceive will lead to a 'fight' or a conflict? Some people use avoidance, as a way of communicating, hoping that if it is not discussed it will go away. Problems not discussed, will not disappear. They will escalate. If you or your partner feels that discussing a problem will intensify into a fight, you might need to consider getting a third party involved in your discussion.

5. Am I emotionally mature enough and ready to get married?

A person who is emotionally mature is able to control their emotions. They are able to control their thoughts and see issues from different perspectives. They do not react in an overly impulsive way. An emotionally mature person has the ability to change negative, irrational, and demeaning thoughts to positive, rational, and uplifting ones. They train themselves to be their own therapist. Have you ever found yourself worrying if someone likes you or if you said something correctly, and then it hits you…*So what if they don't like me? So what if I said something incorrectly? What's done is done; life goes on.* By doing this, you show that you have control over your emotions. To determine your emotional maturity level, go to <u>www.personalityone.com/emotional-maturity-test.html</u>. If you discover that you are not as emotionally mature as you think you are or should be, do something about it. Engage in activities to build your self-esteem. Recognize your strengths and weaknesses. Use your strengths to help others and work on your weaknesses.

6. What is/was his father or father figure like as a husband and a father?

If your future husband's father is alive, get to know him. You'll be surprised at how much you will learn about him. If his father is deceased, ask questions. Parents and grandparents help us to understand who we are. The debate still rages as to whether heredity or environment contributes to a person's behavior. However, what is known is that a combination of both factors helps to shape our personality. Behavioral geneticist David Reiss and his colleagues from George Washington University conducted a thorough and long-term study on the effects of genetics on personality. The results of their study revealed "that genetic influences are largely responsible for how adjusted kids are; how well they do in school, how they get along with their peers, whether they engage in dangerous or delinquent behavior." There is, therefore, some merit to understanding a person's family background.

We grow into the labels that have been defined for us by our family and those closest to us. If students in a classroom can succeed or fail based on the teacher's expectations, think of the effect of families on the lives of children. However, there are many instances where people are determined to overcome the negative traits/behaviors they may have inherited from their parents or from others in their environment. This determination allows them to redefine themselves. Give yourself time (there's that word again) to get to know the other person's background. If you discover skeletons in the closet, communicate with each other and work on these issues. Don't be the person's therapist, but encourage them to seek the help of one if that becomes necessary.

7. What kind of relationship does he have or had with his mother or the dominant female in his life?

What kind of person is his mother? Does he seek to make her happy? Is he committed in his duties to her? Is he respectful and kind to her? If he is respectful to his mother he will surely respect you. Does he treat his mother with kindness and tenderness? Is he patient with her? If you can answer positively to these questions than he will treat you in the same manner. He may very well be someone that you could walk down the aisle with.

8. Does he inspire me to be my best self?

Is it always about him? Do you find that when you share what you have done, he responds by talking about what he has done and completely ignores your comment? This shows a level of selfishness that could be a problem in the future. It may be that he is very self-absorbed and may be threatened by your accomplishments, and therefore, would not want to share in them. In the Bible we are encouraged to be an inspiration to others. The apostle Paul in Hebrews Chapter 10 says that, *We should encourage one another to do good works.*

9. Do we have a history of conflict in our relationship?

Conflict during dating can be likened to a virus that may resurface in the marriage and erode the coupe's bond, making the relationship vulnerable. A well-known British couple dated for five years before they broke up. It was reported that they had reached an "amicable agreement to separate." It was rumored that they had grown apart. Whatever the truth about the separation, we may never know, but we do know that it was significant enough for them to break-up and issue a public announcement. The separation obviously stemmed from some sort of conflict in their relationship. They got back together and decided to get married (in a very elaborate and public ceremony). If they did not adequately resolve this conflict prior to their marriage they may have to deal with some of the same issues in their marriage.

10. Do I think that I will be happier once I'm married?

_____

_____

_____

_____

_____

_____

_____

_____

If your answer to this question is yes, then you may not be ready to get married. Happiness is an emotional state that has eluded human beings for centuries. Money cannot buy happiness. Education cannot buy happiness. Marriage cannot buy happiness. Happiness comes from within. We choose to be happy. Happiness is a feeling of contentment and satisfaction with one's self and one's situation in life. We expect things to make us happy. They will not. Happiness is a general state of enjoyment of one's life. This does not mean that you will not have moments of discontentment, but generally you will have more happy days than unhappy days. A truly happy person is someone others want to be around. Research from the University of Virginia in 2007 found that happy people were more likely to get married than unhappy people. Marriage, therefore, may not make you happier (or happy at all) unless you are a happy person by nature.

11. Do I trust my partner?

All healthy relationships are built on trust. If you have any reason to mistrust that special someone, you need to deal with it immediately. Make sure that you discuss it. The other person needs to know that they have to build/rebuild your trust. If after trying, you still feel a sense of mistrust, then you may have to move on. Strong, long-lasting relationships cannot be built on mistrust. Trust is a two-way street. In addition to a person being trustworthy, you need to be able to trust other people. Some people have difficulty trusting others because of certain experiences in their past. If that is the case with you, it maybe wise to seek help.

12. Do I spend enough quality time with my partner?

Many couples get married and go on to have successful marriages after only knowing each other for a short time. With the invention of the Internet, more couples are engaging in online dating and getting married after a brief courtship. Research shows that online dating can be a useful tool to finding a lifetime partner. My view is that if someone is honestly seeking to find a lifetime partner, he or she will be honest about their appearance, their job, their background, and other details of that nature, because they know that eventually they will have to meet with the other person. Therefore, if two honest people happen to connect and they like each other, it could work out well.

Whether you first meet online or face-to-face, it is important that you get to know the person whom you wish to marry before you make a long-term commitment. Long-distance relationships do not give a couple many opportunities to get to know each other. When Sally dated Harry, he lived eight hours away. They spent the occasional weekend together (not under the same roof, of course), and some public holidays. When they met, their main focus was expressing their love to each other. They spent most of their time together and neglected their friends and family members, from whom they could have learned a lot about each other. Their times together were magical. However, they did not spend time engaging in everyday things. This would have given them the opportunity to get to know each other better.

13. Is this what God wants for my life?

Remember, God's will can be found in the advice of the people around you. There are times when they may not be honest about how they feel for fear of hurting your feelings, so learn to read between the lines. God reveals his will to us in many ways. Ask yourself, *Will this union help me to become a better Christian? Will it draw me closer to Christ? Will it make me a more useful person in my circle of influence?* Be open to his leading.

14. How is my relationship with Christ?

Whether we want to or not, we each have a relationship with Christ; the difference maybe in the type of relationship. Just like with our earthly father, we have a relationship with our Heavenly Father. This relationship may be estranged or it may be intimate. The type of father Christ is to us will depend on the time we spend with him and our desire to open our hearts to him. Coming to terms with the kind of relationship that we have with God could be the stepping-stone to improving that relationship. Recognizing that we need to have a close intimate connection with Our Father in Heaven is a launching pad for a successful and long-lasting marital experience.

R ichard's college sweetheart, Megan, graciously dumped him when he was a sophomore in college. He was devastated. In his junior year he met Melanie, who later became his wife. Ten years later, he met Megan again at a church function. She shared with him that she was recently divorced. She proceeded to share very intimate details of the breakup and shared openly that she had been unfaithful to her husband. In retelling his meeting with Megan to his wife, Richard came to the realization that it was a blessing that Megan had dumped him. If Richard had married Megan, they may have stayed married for many years, but the marriage may have required more work than his marriage to Melanie.

My dear friend, choose wisely. The success of your marriage affects your life on this Earth and your opportunity to be a part of the New Earth to come. God invented marriage as the avenue to bring together male and female as one. Our job is to ensure that we take the time, with the help of God, to choose the one that we can happily spend the rest of our lives with.

I am not advocating that you not marry the person you love because they fall short in any area—quite the contrary. You need to use what you have discovered as a tool for discussion before you get married. Make decisions, promises, and pledges to each other. Write them down and include them as part of your private marriage vows.

My prayer is that the information presented here will help you to choose the right person for you. Use your mind and your heart; do not let your heart rule your mind.

God bless you in your journey to find your lifelong partner.

Before you walk down the aisle, and say "I do," promise yourself that you will:

- Invite God into your heart so that he will be the center of your joy
- Be open to the issues that you will face and make the right choice with God's help
- Keep the lines of communication open and honest between those in your sphere of influence
- Be willing to heed the advice of others
- Walk away from a relationship if that is required for true happiness

_____   _____

Signature   Signature

The "Me" in Marriage

Ms. Tara Parker-Pope wrote a piece recently in the *New York Times* entitled "The Happy Marriage is the 'Me' Marriage." In her article she refers to a study conducted at Monmouth University in New Jersey, where "Research shows that the more self-expansion people experience from their partner, the more committed and satisfied they are in the relationship." In other words, if you are able to grow in your relationship, you will be happier. Husband and wife do not always need to engage in the same activities but can do different things and share these experiences with each other.

I would like to add my views on Ms. Parker-Pope's piece. The letters M and E are at the beginning and the end of the word "marriage", spell the word "me." This could be an indication that even in a marital union, the sense of "me" is very important. Without the "me" in marriage, there is no foundation on which to build a relationship. The more fulfilled we are as individuals, the more fulfilled our marriage will be.

ACKNOWLEDGEMENT

To my loving husband for his love, support and inspiration. And to My Lord and Savior Jesus Christ. He has led me on this journey called life so that I can experience his mercy and love. To Him be Glory and Honor, now and forever more. Amen.

Notes

Introduction

1. Jennifer Baker, *Fact Sheet on Marriage and Divorce in America*,(Forest Institute of Professional Psychology in Springfield, Missouri, Real Relations Solutions, 2007)

2. Author Unknown, *A woman's guide to love and lasting relationships* http://propercourse.blogspot.com/2011/02/womans-guide-to-love-and-lasting.html

Chapter 1

1. United States Department of Health and Human Services report of 2010. http://www.acf.hhs.gov/programs/cb/

Chapter 2

1. Merriam-Webster's Online Dictionary http://www.merriam-webster.com/dictionary/love?show=0&t=1312514430

2. The story of a blind girl, http://academictips.org/blogs/moral-tale-the-story-of-a-blind-girl/

3. Gary Chapman, *The Five Love Languages: How to Express Heartfelt Commitment to your mate*(Northfield Publishing, 1995), 15

Chapter 3

1. Facts and Statistics about infidelity, http://www.truthaboutdeception.com/cheating-and-infidelity/stats-about-infidelity.html (see research by Buss and Shackelford)

2. Mercy Me, 'Beautiful', http://youtu.be/Z6pS5HCkgPI

3. Bruno Mars, 'Just the Way you Are', http://youtu.be/LjhCEhWiKXk

4. Nancy Missler, Faith in the Night Seasons, http://www.khouse. org/articles/1999/234/

5. Author Unknown, *A love story*, http

6. Aesop's fable: *North Wind and the Sun* http://www.storyarts.org/library/aesops/stories/north. html

7. Stephen and Alex Kendrick,(*The Love Dare* Nashville: Broadman and Holman 2008),

8. Marita Littauer, *Wired that Way*(California: Regal Books, 2006), .

9. Tim LaHaye, *Spirit-Controlled Temperament* (California: Tyndale,1994), .

10. Florence Littauer, *The Gift of Encouraging Words*(Nashville: Word, 1995), .

11. Myers Briggs, http://www.myersbriggs.org/my-mbti-personality-type/mbti-basics/

Chapter 4

1. Ted Hudson, http://www.psychologytoday.com/articles/200307/the-success-marriage

2. David Weiss, The Effects of Heredity and Environment on Personality,

3. http://www.scribd.com/doc/45598815/Effects-of-heredity-and-environment-on-development-of-personality (page 38 David Weiss)

4. The National Marriage Project, University of Virginia, http://www.virginia.edu/marriageproject/

Epilogue

1. Tara Parker-Pope, *The Happy Marriage Is the 'Me' Marriage,* The New York Times. http://www.nytimes.com/2011/01/02/weekinreview/02parkerpope.html

.